George Edward Sears

A collection of works illustrative of the Dance of death in the library of George Edward Sears

George Edward Sears

A collection of works illustrative of the Dance of death in the library of George Edward Sears

ISBN/EAN: 9783741135453

Manufactured in Europe, USA, Canada, Australia, Japa

Cover: Foto ©Thomas Meinert / pixelio.de

Manufactured and distributed by brebook publishing software (www.brebook.com)

George Edward Sears

A collection of works illustrative of the Dance of death in the library of George Edward Sears

A

Collection of Works

Illuſtrative of

Ꞇꝓe Ɗance of Ɗeatꝓ

LA DANSE MACABRE   LES IMAGES DE LA MORT
IMAGINES MORTIS   LE TRIOMPHE DE LA MORT
ICONES MORTIS   DER TODTEN TANZ.

IN THE LIBRARY OF

GEORGE EDWARD SEARS

———//———

With Photographic Reproductions of
Rare and Curious Title-Pages and Plates
Selected Therefrom

———//———

New York
PRIVATELY PRINTED
1889

Geo. Edw? Sears:

Artists and Engravers

HANS HOLBEIN,	HANS LÜTZELBERGER,
H. ALDEGREVER,	DAVID DENECKER,
EBERH. KIESER,	JOBST DENECKER,
JOBST AMMAN,	ANTON SYLVIUS,
WENCESLAS HOLLAR.	OTHO VÆNIUS,
CH. DE MECHEL,	MATT. MERIAN,
ANDRÉ TROST,	M. RENTZ,
RUDOLPH MEYER,	CONRAD MEYER,
I. R. SCHELLENBERG,	CALLOT,
CHODOWIECKI,	GEO. CRUIKSHANK,
GRANDVILLE,	D. DEUCHAR,
T. ROWLANDSON,	THOS. BEWICK.
R. DAGLEY,	M. FRENZEL,
J. SCHLOTTHAUER,	BYFIELD,
BONNER,	ALEX. ANDERSON.

The Dance of Death.

NAME given to a certain class of allegorical representations, illustrative of the universal power of Death, and dating from the fourteenth century. When the introduction of Christianity first banished the ancient Germanic conception of a future state, a new description of death mythology arose, partly out of Biblical sources, partly out of the popular character itself, wherein the Last Enemy was represented under simple and majestic images, such as that of a husbandman watering the ground with blood, plowing it with swords, rooting out weeds, plucking up flowers, or felling trees, sowing it with corpses; or, of a monarch assembling his armies, making war, taking prisoners, inviting his subjects to a festival, or citing them to judgment. But with a gradual change in national manners came a change in the mode of treating the subject, and it was associated with every-day images, such as the confessional, chess playing, and, above all, with the adjuncts of a festival, viz., music and dancing. This tendency to familiarize the theme increased during the confusion and turmoil of the fourteenth century, when the national mind alternated between fits of devotion and license, or blent both elements in satire and humor. Such a mood as this naturally occupied itself with personifying Death, and adopted by preference the most startling and grotesque images it could find—that of a musician playing to dancing men, or a dancer leading them on; and as the dance and drama were then intimately connected, and employed on religious occasions, this particular idea soon assumed a dramatic form. This drama was most simply constructed, consisting of short dialogues between Death and "four-and-twenty" or more followers, and was undoubtedly enacted in or near churches by religious orders in Germany during the fourteenth century, and at a rather later period in France.—*Cyclopedia*.

INTRODUCTORY.

Origin of the Subject. The Dance of Death most probably had its origin in the ancient custom of dancing in churches and church-yards, often conducted in an indecorous and ludicrous manner, and which at times assumed the form of a spiritual or religious masquerade, in which Death was, morally, the leading character. These pageants are known to have frequently occurred, even so late as the middle of the fifteenth century in France.

The Early Paintings. Out of this doubtless grew the many varied representations of the subject, painted or sculptured upon the walls of numerous churches, chapels, nunneries, convents, and bridges in France, Germany, Switzerland, and other continental countries, as well as in some parts of England. The earliest known series are believed to be those that were executed in a nunnery near Basle about 1312. Another series were painted in a church in Basle about 1430–50 (now designated as the Gross-Baseler Todtentanz), copies of both of which were fortunately engraved before their destruction, and to which further allusion will be made. The emperors and pontiffs may have ordered these various paintings, or encouraged their execution, to gradually draw the people away from the offensive fooleries of earlier times, as well as for the purpose of awakening a deeper religious spirit among the masses. Be this as it may, the painters with a quiet sarcasm seem to have made no exception in favor of the high and mighty rulers of church and state, and the grim, gaunt skeleton was pictured as leading the Pope, the Emperor, and the King with the same power as when grasping the form of the wretched beggar.

While these numerous frescoes and sculptures were all more or less varied in design, the same ruling idea permeated all, namely, Death as a skeleton, but full of life and frolic, in the act of leading all the different ranks and conditions of mankind, and most frequently in the attitude of a dancing, lively motion.

In some cases, verses of a religious and moral character were painted underneath. No reliable testimony has thus far been given, nor any records found, by which it can be known who the artists were who first executed these frescoes. There is certain evidence, however, that one Klauber, an eminent painter of Basle, in the year 1568 restored those in the church of that city most skillfully, and added two to the series, one being a portrait of himself, and the other of his wife and child, with the skeleton introduced in each.

At the present day these ancient frescoes have almost entirely disappeared. The last of the Basle paintings were destroyed by the *wise* magistrates about 1805, and a fine series at Strasburg, demolished by the bombardment of that city in 1870.

There still exists upon the arches of an old bridge at Luzerne a set of old pictures of the subject, probably dating back three centuries, and a few remnants of others may, without question, be found elsewhere, but if so, sadly defaced and almost obliterated by the ravages of time and want of repairs and restorations.

Early Printed Works.

Shortly after the discovery of Printing, a few works were issued in Paris, called "La Danse Macabre," "La Grant Danse Macabre," etc., with crude and curious wood-cuts, surely suggested by the ancient pictures, accompanied by text in verses, in which a dialogue was carried on between Death and each of his various victims.

The origin and meaning of this word Macabre, or Maccabe, have been the subject of much research by the bibliographers of the present century, to whose works those feeling any interest are referred.

These singular productions of early typography and engraving are now among the most rare and costly gems in the libraries of the curious. Later editions appeared, from the same blocks, for more than a century afterwards, with variations and additions.

In the well known and beautiful Horæ, or Books of Hours, issued at Paris by Vostre, Verard, Godard, Kerver, Geoffroy Tory, 1485-1520, the subject was frequently introduced in the borders surrounding every page, engraved with great skill and cleverness. It is now a question with experts whether these borders are not engraved upon metal, instead of being wood-cuts, as has been the general supposition.

The Holbein Designs.

Not a little interest in this subject, at least so far as the art of engraving upon wood is concerned, centres in the great painter, Hans Holbein. In the early part of the sixteenth century, while a youth, he had, without doubt, closely studied and observed the curious old paintings in his native city of Basle, and became imbued with their spirit. The result was the immortal designs and drawings, which may fairly claim to have been almost entirely new and original, upon the forty-one small wood blocks, engraved by Hans Lützelberger, and which first appeared at Basle, probably about 1525-1530, printed upon one side of sheets, with some text, and in regular book form, at Lyons in 1538. Holbein also about the same

8

period drew a miniature series of the Dance of Death, in the initial letters of the alphabet, which were engraved with great skill and delicacy by Lützelberger.

There is no reliable evidence that Holbein ever painted any series of a Dance of Death in Basle, or that he retouched or restored any of the old frescoes. Some records are preserved which justify the belief that he painted a Death Dance of some kind upon the walls of the old palace of Whitehall during his residence in London, but if so, no trace of such has thus far been found. It would seem that a fair conclusion must be that the old pictures at Basle, executed long before his birth, were the sources of his inspiration at the period he prepared his drawings on the wood.

These original forty-one wood-cuts are even to-day considered the master-pieces of the art. No study of, nor history of the development of wood engraving has been written in which they do not prominently appear, and are recognized as expressing the highest type of genius that the art has yet produced. A few years after the first appearance of the originals, there were issued at Lyons in 1547 editions in the French and Latin text, in which were twelve more cuts, making fifty-three in all, and also an edition dated 1562, containing in all fifty-eight cuts. It is quite probable that Holbein also designed most of these later ones—possibly some are doubtful. Several other issues from the original blocks appeared during the ensuing twenty years, with verses and copious text, sometimes in the French, and again in the Latin language. All of these issues, especially the earlier ones, are quite rare and costly.

Copies of Holbein's Cuts on Wood. No sooner had these remarkable designs appeared, when other artists in various countries made copies of the same, and numerous pirated or surreptitious editions, with these imitations, were published in Venice, Cologne, Basle, and elsewhere. These copies were remarkably clever, more especially those made by an unknown Italian engraver for Valgresi's issue at Venice, 1545, which are by far the best ever executed.

The Birckmanns, celebrated printers of Cologne, issued several pirated copies, the first in 1555, in which all the cuts were reversed, except one, and of a little larger size than the original. Some of these have the monogram $\mathcal{A}^2$, and are attributed to a well-known engraver of the time, Anton Sylvius. Though cleverly executed, they are far inferior to the originals. Jobst DeNecker made very skillful imitations in an edition put forth at Augsburgh in 1544, adding an original one, called "The Adulterer." In the present century Bewick engraved very creditable copies, and Bonner and Byfield, two gifted English artists, made an admirable series for Mr. Douce's "Dissertation." Dr. Alexander Anderson, the father of wood engraving in America, engraved copies similar to Bewick's in 1810, probably the only complete set ever executed in the New World.

Copies upon Copper. During the seventeenth century the copper-plate and metal engravers of Germany and elsewhere seized the subject as portrayed by Holbein. An edition, without date, name or place, but issued at Frankfort sometime between 1590 and 1610, appeared, with a fine frontispiece and sixty copper-plates, surrounded with pretty borders of flowers and fruits, engraved by Eberhard Kieser. All the original designs are copied and several new and curious ones added. These are the first known complete set of copies upon copper. A reproduction of the title-page and of one of the new cuts will be found herein. About 1650 Hollar made his remarkable etchings after Holbein, the beautiful borders being engraved by Diepenbecke. These plates afterwards by some means came into the possession of Mr. Edwards, a London publisher, who about the year 1790–1794 reissued them, without the borders, accompanied by text both in English and French. In 1780 C. De Mechel, of Basle, produced a very beautiful set of copies.

Other Designs upon Copper, with Hints from Holbein. While Kieser, Hollar and De Mechel confined themselves very closely to the actual designs of Holbein, very many other editions appeared during the seventeenth and eighteenth, as well as present century, in which the engravers, while largely borrowing from the great originals, and in a marked degree embodying their main features, yet added many new and curious designs, in which the manners, customs and follies of the time were satirized, and which were often of a comical and humorous character. These plates were almost always accompanied by texts, discourses, pious and secular verses, dialogues, songs of Death, set to appropriate music, etc., etc.

Copies of the Old Basle Paintings. In the early part of the seventeenth century, Mattheu Merian, a celebrated engraver of Frankfort, very fortunately made copies of the old pictures in the church at Basle, which were shortly afterwards almost obliterated, and, as before stated, destroyed about 1805. These copies he engraved upon copper in a masterly manner, and they were first issued in book form at Frankfort in the year 1649, with accompanying text in German, followed by several later editions, some having the text in both French and German. A fac-simile of the title-page of this early issue and of one of the cuts of this series is here presented.

There is some reason to believe that a portion, at least, of the old pictures had also been copied and engraved upon wood previous to the year 1600. In a reprint in this collection, dated Basle, 1796, there are several wood-cuts of the Basle Dance, upon one of which there is the mark G. S., with a graver's tool underneath, and dated 1576. If this was the original block, it would prove that fact, but possibly some deception may have been practiced.

Modern Reproductions. In recent years many very creditable reprints and fac-similes of the Danse Macabre, the Holbein cuts, Hollar's and De Mechel's etchings, the Basle Dance, Merian's plates, etc., etc., have been published, and can be secured at very moderate outlay. The etchings after Holbein, by Frenzel, Leipzig, 1831, and those lithographed by Prof. Schlotthauer, Munich, 1832, are admirably executed. Many of the very rare and costly early French issues of " La Danse Macabre " have also been cleverly reproduced by the Plinski process, at Paris, while the German publishers have given faithful copies after Merian, Hollar, and De Mechel.

Bibliography. The bibliography of the subject may be said to date from the past half century, and is amply and fully represented by the labors of Piegnot, Kastner, Langlois, Dufour, and others in France; by Massmann, Edel, Lippmann in Germany, and Douce and Humphreys in England. To the above studies and dissertations the curious inquirer is referred. Many of these works contain very valuable and interesting plates and fac-similes, and the subject matter evinces thorough research and study into the various phases of this curious and fascinating theme.

Summary. After this somewhat hurried outline, it may be mentioned that this sombre Death Dance has been treated in every variety of form and feature that the lively fancy and thoughtful study of artists, painters, poets, scholars and satirists could suggest. It has permeated the literature of the past four centuries; more especially is it always found in some guise in the innumerable emblem books of the sixteenth and seventeenth centuries. In our own day it has been illustrated by the clever pencils of Rowlandson, Deuchar, Dagley, Cruikshank, Bewick and Grandville, not forgetting our American Bewick, the late Dr. Anderson. The photographic reproductions accompanying this catalogue give but a slight idea of the varied forms in which the subject was treated; and, so far as known, the most of them appear here for the first time. In nearly every case they have been taken directly from the originals, and may therefore be relied upon for accuracy.

In the gradual formation of a collection of books intended to illustrate the origin, growth and development of the arts of printing and engraving, it seemed essential that this most important feature should be fairly represented; and this, together with a study of Mr. Douce's valuable work, and Peignot's researches, inspired a wish to secure what might be obtainable of these literary and artistic curios.

The collection herein described, though very far from completion, and much yet to be secured if time and opportunity are vouchsafed, has, however, largely gratified the desire and given zest and variety to many leisure hours of the past ten years. It may also possibly be fairly entitled to the credit of forming a modest link in the chain of rare and valuable acquisitions secured in recent years from the shelves of the old world by our amateur collectors.

NEW YORK,   1889.   G. E. S.

PLATE II.

Il y a vne voye, qui semble droicte deuant l'homme:
mais la fin q'icelle mene à la mort.

PROVER. XIIII.

Telle voye aux humains est bonne,
Et à l'homme trespuisse semble:
Mais la fin d'elle à l'homme donne,
La MORT, qui tous pecheurs assemble.

The Nun:
FROM HOLBEIN,
In "Les Images de la la Mort."
Lyons, 1547.
*

SCENE:—A Covered Bridge at Lucerne.

Elsie.—   How dark it grows!
What are these paintings on the walls around us?

Prince Henry.—The Dance Macaber!

Elsie.—What?

Prince Henry.—The Dance of Death!
All that go to and fro must look upon it,
Mindful of what they shall be, while beneath,
Among the wooden piles, the turbulent river
Rushes, impetuous as the river of life,
With dimpling eddies ever green and bright,
Save where the shadow of this bridge falls on it.

Elsie.—O, yes! I see it now!

Prince Henry.—   The grim musician
Leads all men through the mazes of that dance,
To different sounds in different measures moving;
Sometimes he plays a lute, sometimes a drum,
To tempt or terrify.

Elsie.—What is this picture?

Prince Henry.—It is a young man singing to a nun
Who kneels at her devotions, but in kneeling

18

Turns round to look at him, and Death meanwhile,
Is putting out the candles on the altar!
　　Here he has stolen a jester's cap and bells,
And dances with the Queen.
　　And here the heart of the new-wedded wife,
Coming from church with her beloved lord,
He startles with the rattle of his drum.
　　　　Under it is written,
"Nothing but Death shall separate thee and me!"

　　Elsie.—And what is this that follows close upon it?

　　Prince Henry.—Death, playing on a dulcimer.
　　　　Behind him,
A poor old woman, with a rosary,
Follows the sound and seems to wish her feet
Were swifter to o'ertake him. Underneath,
The inscription reads, "Better is Death than Life."

　　Elsie.—Better is Death than Life! Ah yes! to
　　　　thousands
Death plays upon a dulcimer, and sings
That song of consolation, till the air
Rings with it, and they cannot choose but follow
Whither he leads. And not the old alone
But the young also hear it, and are still.

　　Prince Henry.—Let us go forward, and no longer stay
In this great picture-gallery of Death!
I hate it! ay, the very thought of it!

　　Elsie.—Why is it hateful to you?

　　Prince Henry.—　　　　For the reason
That life, and all that speaks of life, is lovely,
And Death, and all that speaks of Death, is hateful.

　　Elsie.—The grave itself is but a covered bridge,
Leading from light to light, through a brief darkness!

BIBLIOGRAPHICAL WORKS

RELATING TO THE SUBJECT

DOUCE (Francis). The Dance of Death exhibited in elegant engravings on wood, with a dissertation on the several representations of that subject, etc. *London*, (PICKERING), 1833, 8vo., *half calf, gilt back, marbled edges.* FIRST EDITION, SCARCE.

₊ Contains a very fine set of fac-similes of the Holbein cuts, upon wood, by Bonner and Byfield. Mr. Douce's valuable dissertation is a recognized authority on many disputed points.

DOUCE (Francis). Holbein's Dance of Death, exhibited in elegant engravings on wood, with a dissertation, etc.; also, Holbein's Bible cuts, consisting of 90 illustrations on wood, with introduction by Thos. Frognall Dibdin. *London*, (BOHN), 1858, 12mo., *cloth*, UNCUT.

₊ A later and inexpensive reprint of Mr. Douce's dissertation, with copies of Holbein's Bible cuts, added, etc.

DUFOUR (L'Abbé Valentin). La Danse Macabre peinte en 1425 au Cimetière des Innocents. Fac-simile de l'edition 1484 Précédé de Recherches par L'Abbé Valentin Dufour. *Paris*, (WILLEM), 1875, large 4to, *broche*, UNCUT, *only 250 copies printed sur papier vergé teinté*, EPUISÈ.

₊ This valuable treatise by Dufour, has an elegant etched frontispiece of an ancient painting of the Dance of Death, by Lenoir; also, a fac-simile of an edition of the Danse Macabre, 1484.

EDEL (Fr. W.) Die Neue Kirche in Strassburg. Nachrichten von ihrer entstehung, ihren schicksalen und merkwürdigkeiten, bes. auch vom neuentdeckten Todtentanze. *Strassburg*, 1825, 8vo., *half red morocco, gilt top edges*, UNCUT, RARE.

₊ Contains copies of the Dance of Death, painted on the walls of the old Dominican Convent at Strassburg, now entirely destroyed by the bombardment of the city in 1870.

FORTOUL (Hippolytye). La Danse des Morts dessinée par Hans Holbein, gravée sur pierre par Joseph Schlotthauer, epliqueé par Hippolytye Fortoul. *Paris, n. d.,* (1842), Small 4to, *half calf, gilt top edges,* UNCUT, SCARCE.

₊ M. Fortoul has given a very complete study of the subject, and also a fac-simile of the title-page and preface to first edition issued at Lyons, 1538, and a complete fac-simile of the first edition at Basle, 1554. The copies of the 53 cuts, by Schlotthauer, of Munich, are among the finest of the modern reproductions of Holbein's cuts.

HUMPHREYS (H. N.) Hans Holbein's celebrated Dance of Death, illustrated by a series of photo-lithographic fac-similes from a copy of the first edition, now in the British Museum, etc. *London,* (QUARITCH), 1868, 12mo., *cloth, red edges.*

JUBINAL (Achille). Explication de la danse des morts de la Chaise-Dieu, fresque inédite due quinzième siecle, précédée de quelques detail sur les autres monumens de ce genre. Avec quatre figures en couleur. *Paris,* 1841, large 4to, *half morocco,* UNCUT, SCARCE.

₊ This work gives an account of the frescoes of the Danse Macaber, on the walls of an old church at Auvergne, in France, also very fine copies of same, in colors. Autograph letters of the author are inserted in the present copy.

KASTNER (Georges). Les Danses des Morts, dissertations et recherches, historiques, philosophiques, littéraires et musicales sur les divers monuments de ce genre qui existent ou qui ont existé tant en France qu'a L'Etranger, accompagnées de La Danse Macabre, etc., etc., *Paris,* 1852, large 4to, *half morocco, gilt top edges,* UNCUT, VERY SCARCE.

₊ Contains nearly 200 beautiful fac-similes and original designs not found elsewhere. The musical researches are especially valuable.

LANGLOIS (E. H.) Essai historique, philosophique, et pittoresque, sur les danses de morts, etc. *Rouen,* 1852, 2 vols., 8vo., *half calf, gilt top edges,* UNCUT, VERY FINE COPY.

₊ This able work contains several fine fac-similes of the various old paintings; a few of Holbein's designs, and others new and curious. Also, a valuable list of editions, their titles, dates, etc.

MERINO (A. Fernandez). La Danza Macabre, estudio, critico, literario. *Madrid,* 1884, 8vo., *broché,* UNCUT.

₊ A recent critical essay on the Macabre Dance, issued in Spain.

MASSMAN (H. F.) Die Baseler Todtentänze in getreuen abbildungen, nebst geschichtlicher untersuchung, sowie vergleichung mit den übrigen deutschen Todtentänzen, ... sammt einem anhange: Todtentanz in Holzschnitten des fünfzehnten Jahrhunderts von H. F. Massman. *Stuttgart,* 1847, 2 vols., Text, in 8vo., Atlas, in 4to., *with eighty-one engravings upon twenty-two copper-plates; also, twenty-seven fac-similes from early Block-Books, half morocco, gilt top edges,* UNCUT.

⁎ Massman gives complete copies of the old paintings at Basle, after Merian and Buchel, a valuable list of various editions of works on the Dance of Death, etc., etc.

PEIGNOT (Gabriel). Recherches historiques sur les danses des morts et sur l'origine des cartes a jouer, ouvrage orné de cinq lithographies et de vignettes, par Gabriel Peignot. *Dijon,* 1826, 8vo., *half calf, sprinkled edges,* VERY SCARCE.

⁎ It is enough to know that Mons. Peignot gave this subject his thought and attention to be assured that his researches are of great value. There are several plates and fac-similes in the work.

SCHLOTTHAUER (J.) Hans Holbein's Todtentanz in 53 getreu nach den Holzschnitten lithographirten blättern, Herausgegeben von J. Schlotthauer, etc. *Munchen,* 1832, 12mo., *half vellum,* UNCUT, SCARCE, FIRST IMPRESSIONS.

⁎ In this volume are the 53 Holbein cuts so cleverly lithographed, as almost to be mistaken for the wood originals, accompanied by bibliographical and literary remarks on the Dance of Death, by Massman and Schubert. These plates were afterwards used in later editions by Fortoul, (1842); Smith, (1849).

SCHULTZ JACOBI (J. C.) De Nederlandsche Doodendans. *Utrecht,* 1849, 8vo., *half morocco, gilt top, folding plates.*

⁎ An interesting monograph on several rare Editions of the Dance of Death, printed in the Netherlands.

SMITH (J. Russell). Holbein's Dance of Death, with an historical and literary introduction. *London,* 1849, small 8vo., *full morocco, gilt edges,* FINE COPY.

⁎ The fac-simile plates in this work are by Schlotthauer, of Munich, engraved upon stone in a masterly manner, beautiful impressions.

VALLARDI (G.) Trionfo e danza della morte, o danza Macabra a Clusone, dogma della morte a pisogne nella provincia de Bergamo, etc., etc. *Milan,* 1859, imp. 8vo., *boards,* UNCUT, VERY SCARCE.

⁎ Contains several folding plates, one beautifully colored, of Death and Childhood.

17

PLATE III.

Title-Page:

Eberh. Kieser's Plates. *Frankfort, circa 1600.*

*

𝕳𝖔𝖑𝖇𝖊𝖎𝖓'𝖘 𝕯𝖆𝖓𝖈𝖊 𝖔𝖋 𝕯𝖊𝖆𝖙𝖍.

EDITIONS, WITH ORIGINAL WOOD-CUTS DESIGNED BY HOLBEIN
AND ENGRAVED BY HANS LÜTZELBERGER.

LYONS, 1547.

Les Images de la Mort, auxquelles sont adioustées douze
figures. Davantage, la médecine de l'ame la consolation des
malades, un sermon de mortalité, etc. *A la fin :* Imprimé à Lyon a
l'escu de Coloigne, par Jehan Frellon, 1547, WITH 53 WOOD-CUTS BY
HOLBEIN. 12mo., *full Levant morocco, elegant binding by* TRAUTZ-
BAUZONNET, VERY RARE, ORIGINAL IMPRESSIONS.

⁎ This is the first edition, containing 53 cuts, the earlier ones having but 41. Being very
fine impressions from the genuine blocks, and equally well printed, if not surpassing the first
issue by the Trechsels in 1538, it is a very desirable example. Most of the modern bibliographers have made use of this issue in reproducing fac-similes. A copy of one of the cuts,
"The Nun," is given herein.

ANTWERP, 1654.

WOLSSCHATEN (G. van).   De Doodt vermaskert met des
weerelts ydelheyt afghedaen door Geeraerdt van Wolsschaten.
Verciert met de constighe Beldher van den vermaerden schilder
Hans Holbeen. (Death masked with the world's vanity, ornamented
with the ingenious images of the famous painter, Holbein.)
Antwerp, 1654, WITH 18 WOOD-CUTS, 14 OF WHICH ARE THE
ORIGINAL BLOCKS RETOUCHED.   Small 8vo., *newly bound, full
maroon calf, gilt top edges by* STIKEMAN, RARE.

⁎ This volume has special interest, as showing the preservation of some of the original
wood-blocks more than a century after their first appearance (about 1530-1538). The monogram
A appears upon some of them, probably to indicate that this engraver of Antwerp, into
whose hands they had fallen, had retouched them. Thought to be the mark of Anton Sylvius.
Douce, pp. 109-110.

19

EDITIONS, WITH COPIES OF THE HOLBEIN CUTS UPON WOOD.

FIRST EDITION OF THE FIRST COPIES. ISSUED

AT VENICE, 1545.

SIMOLACHRI ‖ Historie, E. Figvre ‖ De La Morte. ‖ oue ſi contiene, ‖ La Medicina de L'Anima vtile, ‖ etc : etc : (Printer's device of the brazen serpent.) Con gratia e priuilegio de l'illuftrif Senato ‖ Vinitiano, per anni dicci. ‖ *Appreffo Vincenzo Vaugris al segno d'Erasmo.* MDXLV., WITH 41 REMARKABLY FINE WOOD-CUTS, IMITATING THE MASTER PIECES OF HOLBEIN. 12mo., *full dark olive crushed Levant morocco,* symbolically tooled, by ALFRED MATTHEWS, VERY RARE.

₊ This work is described by Douce (p. 111) as containing the first, and by far the best copies of Holbein's designs. Whoever the artist was, he certainly displayed extraordinary merit, and only an expert could distinguish the slight inferiority. The printer, Valgresi, goes so far as to assert in his preface, that they are finer than the originals. They far excel the copies made in Germany, first issued by Birckmann at Cologne, 1555, ten years later, upon which appear the monogram *A⁹*, which is believed to be that of Anton Sylvius.

———

RARE AND CURIOUS EDITION, ISSUED

AT VENICE, 1596.

GLISSENTI (Fabio). Discorsi morali dell' eccellente Sig. Fabio Glissenti, contra il dispiacer del morire. Detto athanatophilia, divisi in cinque Dialoghi, occorsi in cinque giormate... con trenta vaghi et utili Ragionamenti, come tante piaceuoli Nouelle, etc. *Venetia, Dom. Farri,* 1596, WITH OVER 300 WOOD-CUTS, ILLUSTRATING THE DANCE OF DEATH, INCLUDING COPIES OF THE HOLBEIN SERIES. Thick 4to, *vellum gilt,* UNCUT, VERY TALL, CLEAN COPY, FIRST EDITION, EXTREMELY RARE.

₊ Première édition d'un ouvrage peu connu. C'est une sorte de tragédie de la vie humaine en cinq tableaux, dans lesquels sont comprises trente nouvelles. On trouve dans le courant du volume TROIS CENT QUATRE-VINGT-UNE GRAVURES SUR BOIS, ayant toutes plus ou moins rapport aux Danses des Morts. *(La suite de Holbein y est copiée en entier.)* Le beau portrait de Glissenti, répété 6 fois, est entouré d'emblèmes funèbres, ainsi que la plupart des autres planches.
Exemplaire rempli de temoins en tous sens.
Douce (p. 112) notices an edition of this work dated 1609, and claims for it extreme rarity. This first and earlier issue seems to have escaped him.

PLATE IV.

FROM

Eberh. Kieser's Edition.

Circa 1600.

*

COPIED AFTER HOLBEIN, ENGRAVED UPON WOOD.

COLOGNE, 1555.

𝕴𝖒𝖆𝖌𝖎𝖓𝖊𝖘 𝕸𝖔𝖗𝖙𝖎𝖘; His accesserunt epigrammata è Gallico idiomate à Georgio Æmylio in Latinum translata. Ad haec Medicina Animae, etc. Coloniœ Apud hæredes Arnoldi Birck-manni, Anno 1555, WITH 53 WOOD-CUTS AFTER HOLBEIN. Small 8vo., *full morocco extra*, FIRST EDITION, FINE IMPRESSIONS, RARE.

₊ Douce calls this a pirated edition, copied from the Lyons Issue of 1547. The size of the cuts is somewhat larger than the originals, and all are reversed, save one. The mark *A*² appears on a few, supposed to be the monogram of Anton Sylvius. The two demons in the cut of the Pope are left out. In the Soldier, the thigh-bone in the hand of Death is altered to a spear. As a whole they are creditable, but greatly inferior to the masterpieces. Douce, pp. 113-114. Peignot, p. 60. Langlois, Tom. II., p. 118.

NUREMBERG, 1560.

𝕯𝖊𝖗 𝕿𝖔𝖉𝖙𝖊𝖓𝖉𝖆𝖓𝖙𝖟 durch alle Stende vnd Geschlecht der Menschen, darinnen jr herkommen vnd ende, nichtigkeit vnd sterbligkeit als in einem Spiegel zu beschawen, fürgebildet, vnnd mit schönen Figuren gezieret (herausgegeben von *Caspar Scheyt*) S. L. (Nuremberg), Im Jar MDLX., WITH 53 WOOD-CUTS AFTER HOLBEIN. Small 8vo., *full morocco, gilt top edges, by* ALFRED MATTHEWS. FINE COPY, VERY RARE.

₊ These cuts appear very coarsely executed, although the same mark *A*² appears on a few. The text is in German by Gaspard Scheyt. Langlois, Tom. II., p. 110. Not cited by Douce.

COLOGNE, 1567.

𝕴𝖒𝖆𝖌𝖎𝖓𝖊𝖘 𝕸𝖔𝖗𝖙𝖎𝖘, his accesserunt epigrammata è Gallico idiomate à Georgio Æmylio in Latinum translata. Ad haec Medi-cina Animæ, etc. Coloniœ Apud hæredes Arnoldi Birckmanni, Anno 1567, WITH 53 WOOD-CUTS AFTER HOLBEIN. Small 8vo., *interesting contemporary binding, old stamped pigskin*, RARE.

₊ This is simply a later issue of Birckmann's 1555 edition, and in all respects similar, calling for no further remark.

WITTEMBERG, 1590.

CHYTRÆI.—Libellvs Davidis Chytræi de morte et vita æterna, editio postrema cui additæ sunt Imagines Mortis, illustratæ epi-grammatis D. Georgii Æmilli [wood-cut of a skull]. Witebergæ, Impressus à Matthæo Welack. Anno MDXC., WITH 53 WOOD-CUTS COPIED AFTER HOLBEIN. Small thick 8vo., *vellum*, FINE CLEAR IMPRESSIONS, VERY SCARCE.

₊ In the middle of this rare book, preceded by another title-page, " Imagines Mortis," etc., are found copies of the Holbein designs, evidently by other engravers. Some have the mark ✝ and one the mark \X/ with a graver underneath. Langlois, Tom. II., p. 122. Douce, p. 117.

LONDON, 1789.

𝕰𝖒𝖇𝖑𝖊𝖒𝖘 𝖔𝖋 𝕸𝖔𝖗𝖙𝖆𝖑𝖎𝖙𝖞, representing in upwards of fifty cuts, Death seizing all ranks and degrees of people, with historical account of paintings on this subject in divers parts of Europe. *London* [printed for T. Hodgson] 1789, WITH 51 WOOD-CUTS OF HOLBEIN BY JOHN BEWICK. Small 8vo., *full blue morocco, extra tooled sides, gilt top edges by* BEDFORD, FIRST EDITION, UNCUT, SCARCE.

*** Douce states these cuts were engraved by the brother of Thomas Bewick, of Newcastle. There is an essay upon the subject added, written by John Sidney Hawkins, Esq. Douce, pp. 118-119.

DR. ANDERSON'S COPIES ON WOOD.

NEW HAVEN, CONN., 1846.

𝕰𝖒𝖇𝖑𝖊𝖒𝖘 𝖔𝖋 𝕸𝖔𝖗𝖙𝖆𝖑𝖎𝖙𝖞, representing by numerous engravings Death seizing all ranks and conditions of people, etc., with an apostrophe to each, translated from the Latin, etc. *Charleston, S. C., New Haven, Ct.*, 1846, WITH WOOD-CUT COPIES AFTER HOLBEIN BY ALEX. ANDERSON, FIRST WOOD ENGRAVER IN AMERICA. Small 12mo., *half calf, gilt top edges,* FINE COPY, UNCUT, SCARCE.

*** These cuts first appeared in an edition at New Haven in 1810, and 36 years later, being found in fine condition, the present issue was put forth. Anderson had evidently secured a copy of Bewick's work, and as an ardent disciple of that school had made his blocks from those copies.

PLATE V.

Title-Page:
Rudolph and Conrad Meyers' Issue.
Zurich, 1650.

*

𝔥𝔬𝔩𝔟𝔢𝔦𝔫'𝔰 𝔇𝔞𝔫𝔠𝔢 𝔬𝔣 𝔇𝔢𝔞𝔱𝔥.

COPIES ENGRAVED IN COPPER.

FRANKFORT, CIRCA 1600.

𝔗𝔬𝔡𝔱𝔢𝔫 𝔇𝔞𝔫𝔱𝔷 durch alle stände und Geschlecht der Menschen, etc., (Death's Dance through all ranks and conditions of men.) s. l. n. d. [*Frankfort circa* 1600], WITH FRONTISPIECE AND 60 COPPER PLATES, INCLUDING COMPLETE SET AFTER HOLBEIN, EN-GRAVED BY EBERH. KIESER. 4to., *original vellum cover, in salander case*, EXCESSIVELY RARE.

*** Probably this is the earliest issue in which the entire Holbein series were engraved upon copper. The plates are within borders of flowers and fruits, accompanied by Scripture texts and verses. Some new and original cuts also appear. The title-page and one of these new designs will be found reproduced in this catalogue. It is a volume of great rarity. Douce, pp. 121-122. Langlois, Tom. II., p. 125.

LAYBACH-SALTZBURG, 1682.

VALVASOR (J. W.) Theatrum mortis humanæ tripartitum. I. Pars. Saltum Mortis. II. Pars. Varia genera Mortis. III. Pars. Pænas Damnatorum continens, cum figuris æneis illustratum (same title repeated in German), etc. Gedrucht zu *Laybach* und zu finden bey Joh. Bap. Mayr, in *Saltzburg*, Anno 1682, WITH FRONTISPIECE AND 54 BEAUTIFUL PLATES OF DANCE OF DEATH AFTER HOLBEIN. ALSO 66 OTHERS, REPRESENTING THE TORTURES OF THE WICKED, ENGRAVED BY ANDRÉ TROST. Small 4to., *full morocco, super extra gilt edges by* DE COVERLY, VERY FINE COPY, FIRST EDITION, RARE.

*** In the first part of this work the artist has engraved very elegant copies of the Holbein series. In the latter part are many frightful and curious designs of Tortures. Dibdin, in his "Bibliographical Decameron," Vol. I., p, 42, notices this work. Also, Douce. pp. 129-130 Langlois, Tom. II., p. 130.

COPIES BY CHRETIEN DE MECHEL.

BASLE, 1780.

𝔏𝔢 𝔗𝔯𝔦𝔬𝔪𝔭𝔥𝔢 𝔡𝔢 𝔩𝔞 𝔐𝔬𝔯𝔱, gravé d'apres les dessins origi-naux de Jean Holbein par Chr. de Mechel graveur à Basle, MDCCLXXX., WITH FRONTISPIECE AND 47 PLATES AFTER HOLBEIN. Royal 4to., *half morocco, gilt top edges*, UNCUT, BRIL-LIANT FIRST IMPRESSIONS, SCARCE.

*** This forms the first part of a collection of Holbein's works, issued and engraved by de Mechel. Mr. Douce gives full details of the work, see pp. 132-135.

Copies by Wenceslaus Hollar.

London, 1794.

The Dance of Death, painted by H. Holbein and engraved by W. Hollar, to which is added The Daunce of Machabree, by Dan John Lydgate, s. l. n. d. [*London*, J. Edwards, 1794], WITH PORTRAITS OF HOLBEIN AND HOLLAR, AND 30 ETCHINGS BY W. HOLLAR AFTER HOLBEIN, 4to., *full calf*, SCARCE.

₊ This title is deceiving, Holbein not known to have painted any series on the subject, but simply to have designed the wood-cuts, of which these are copies.   Hollar probably produced these plates at Antwerp about 1651.   Mr. Edwards, a London bookseller, in some way secured them, had them rebitten, and issued them as above.   These impressions, while very fair, are of course greatly inferior to the first impressions, which were surrounded by elegant borders, engraved by Diepenbecke, and are of excessive rarity and value.   Douce, pp. 125-129.

SAME EDITION, FRENCH TEXT,

PARIS, 1794.

Le Triomphe de la Mort, gravé d'apres les dessins de Holbein par W. Hollar.   Explication des sujets du Triomphe de la Mort de Jean Holbein. s. l. n. d. [*a Paris*, 1794], WITH PORTRAITS OF HOLBEIN AND HOLLAR, AND 30 ETCHINGS BY HOLLAR AFTER HOLBEIN, 4to., *full calf gilt, blind toolings*, VERY SCARCE.

₊ This appears to be exactly similar in all respects to the London edition just described, and was probably issued for the publishers and booksellers of Paris.

LATER EDITIONS—HOLLAR'S ETCHINGS.

LONDON, 1816.

The Dance of Death, from the original designs of Hans Holbein, illustrated with thirty-three plates engraved by W. Hollar, with descriptions in English and French.   *London*, 1816, WITH PORTRAITS AND PLATES BY HOLLAR, 8vo., *half morocco, gilt top edges*, SCARCE.

————

Another copy of same edition, of which a very limited number were issued, WITH THE PLATES FINELY COLORED, 8vo., *fine old English red morocco, gilt toolings, gilt edges*, VERY SCARCE.

₊ These appear to be still later reprints of the same etchings of Hollar, as issued by Mr. Edwards in 1794, with introductory notes and a brief memoir of Holbein.   See Douce, p. 128.

ETCHINGS BY M. FRENZEL.

LEIPZIG, 1831.

BECHSTEIN (L.)   Der Todtentanz, ein gedicht von Ludwig Bechstein, mit 48 kupfern in treuen conturen nach H. Holbein. *Leipzig*, 1831, WITH 48 ETCHINGS AFTER HOLBEIN, BY M. FRENZEL, 8vo., *half vellum, gilt top edges*, UNCUT.

₊ The 48 beautiful etchings in this work were executed by M. Frenzel, Director of the Print Museum at Dresden.   The Poem by Bechstein expresses the power of Death over Humanity.   Douce, pp. 136-7.

24

PLATE VI.

73

33. Roch.

Koch.

Kein speyß gekocht vom Tod befreyt
Das Himel Brodt allein gedyt.
Weil ich der Seelen-speiß duth meiden,
Muß ich ietz Ewig Hunger leiden.

The Cook:

Meyers' Edition. Zurich, 1650.

*

DEUCHAR (D.)   The Dances of Death, through the various
stages of human life, wherein the capriciousness of that tyrant is
exhibited in forty-six copper-plates, done from the original designs,
which were cut in wood and afterwards painted by John Holbein in
the town house at Basle, to which is prefixed descriptions of each
plate in French and English, with the Scripture text from which
the designs were taken.   *London*, 1803, WITH PORTRAIT OF
DEUCHAR, FRONTISPIECE AND 46 ETCHINGS OF HOLBEIN'S DESIGNS,
4to., *half calf*, CLEAR IMPRESSIONS, SCARCE.

⁎ Deuchar followed closely Hollar's copies—some have been copied from the spurious
Cologne editions, with slight variations.   The same inaccuracy is observed in the title,
alluding to the paintings of Holbein.   **The etchings are** much below Hollar's work, but many
are very creditable.   Douce, pp. 135-6.

COPIES BY HELLMUTH.
MAGDEBURG, 1836.

HELLMUTH (C.)   Der Todtentanz oder der Triumpf des Todes,
nach den original Holzschnitten des Hans Holbein, von C. H.
Magdeburg, 1836, WITH ENGRAVED TITLE, AND 46 LITHOGRAPH
COPIES AFTER HOLBEIN.   Large 4to., *half morocco*, CLEAR IMPRES-
SIONS, SCARCE.

⁎ Douce does not notice this work, having most likely been issued **after his own**
dissertation on the subject.   The copies seem to be after the celebrated copies on wood made
by Denecker in 1544, who introduced "The Adulterer" and "Christ on the Cross" to the
series.   This is one of the earliest editions in which copies were made on stone.

MODERN REPRINTS OF DE MECHEL'S COPIES.
PARIS, CIRCA 1860.

𝕷𝖊 𝕿𝖗𝖎𝖔𝖒𝖕𝖍𝖊 𝖉𝖊 𝖑𝖆 𝕸𝖔𝖗𝖙, gravè d'apres les dessins origi-
naux de Holbein, par Chrétien de Mechel, graveur à Bale, 1780.
(Reprint by Simon Racon et Cie.)   *Paris, n. d., circa*, 1860, WITH
48 BEAUTIFUL PLATES OF HOLBEIN'S DANCE OF DEATH, AFTER DE
MECHEL'S COPIES, Small 4to, *full morocco, extra gilt edges*, by
BARDISSER, SCARCE.

⁎ A very fine recent reprint of the copies by de Mechel.   The descriptions of the
plates are upon India paper, and the plates themselves are upon papier velin.   Only a very
limited number were issued.

UTTWEIL, 1858.

𝕯𝖊𝖗 𝕿𝖔𝖉𝖙𝖊𝖓𝖙𝖆𝖓𝖟, von Hans Holbein, nach den originalen ge-
stochen von Chr. von Mechel in Basel, 1780.   *Uttweil*, 1858, WITH
48 COLORED LITHOGRAPHIC PLATES OF DE MECHEL'S COPIES, 4to,
cloth, gilt edges.

Another copy, same plates, but not colored, 4to, *half morocco, gilt back.*

*** These are two inexpensive modern issues with lithographic plates, accompanied by text in German. The plates in both are taken from the de Mechel designs first issued at Basle, 1780.

BERLIN, 1878.

LIPPMANN (F.) Der Todtentanz von Hans Holbein, nach dem exemplare der ersten ausgabe im Kgl. Kupferstich-Cabinet zu Berlin, in Lichtdruck nachgebildet, von Dr. Freidrich Lippmann. *Berlin,* 1878. Small 4to., *half brown morocco, gilt top,* UNCUT, *by* ALFRED MATTHEWS.

*** Contains very meritorious fac-similes of Holbein's designs. Dr. Lippmann has recently issued a very valuable work on Italian Wood Engraving.

RECENT REPRINT OF LYONS ISSUE, 1538.

1884.

Les Simulachres et historiées faces de la Mort avtant elegamment pourtraictes, que artificiellement imaginées. A Lyon, soubz l'escu de *Coloigne,* MDXXXVIII. (Reprinted, 1884), WITH 41 FAC-SIMILES OF THE ORIGINAL HOLBEIN CUTS, 4to, *half light calf, gilt top edges,* UNCUT.

*** A late fac-simile copy of the very rare edition of 1538, in which the 41 wood-cuts of Holbein appeared for the first time in book form. The original edition of 1538 is now of great value and scarcity. This reprint was produced in Germany, is very nicely executed, and quite inexpensive.

LONDON, N. D.

GRIGGS (W.) Holbein's Dance of Death, a photo-lithographic fac-simile by W. Griggs, from the Ottley Collection in the British Museum. *London, n. d.,* Folio, *16 leaves, paper cover.*

*** Mr. Otdey, the well-known writer of the "History of Wood Engraving," possessed a set of the Holbein cuts evidently printed on sheets, one side only, before they appeared in book form; also, other and very early impressions of the Death Alphabet, etc., etc., which he bequeathed to the British Museum. These are fac-similes of the same.

PLATE VII.

Title-Page:

Mattheu Merian's Issue. *Frankfort. 1649.*

Variations.

EDITIONS, WHERE NEW DESIGNS ARE INTRODUCED,
SERIOUS AND COMICAL,

With Hints from Holbein.

ENGRAVINGS BY THE BROTHERS RUDOLPH AND CONRAD MEYER.

ZURICH, 1650.

MEYERS (Rud. and Con.)   Todten-Dantz.   Ergantz et und
herausgegeben durch Conrad Meyern, Maalern in Zurich, im Jahr
1650.   On engraved title, followed by printed title,—Sterbenspiegel,
das ist sonnenklare vorstellung menschlicher nichtigkeit durch alle
Ständ und Geschlechter : vermitlest 60 dienstlicher Kupferblatteren
lehrreicher uberschriften, etc., etc.   (The Mirror of Death, that is,
a brilliant picture of human nothingness, in all ranks and conditions,
moving Songs of Death, etc., etc.)   Getruckt zu *Zurich*, bey Joh.
Jac. Bodmer, MDCL., WITH FRONTISPIECE, AND 60 BEAUTIFUL
COPPER PLATES OF DANCE OF DEATH, 4to, *full crushed levant morocco,
antique by* BRADSTREET, FIRST EDITION, FINE ORIGINAL IMPRESSIONS,
RARE.

₊ Many of the subjects in this work are entirely new and original, while a number
are evidently suggested by Holbein's masterpieces.   A curious feature is the pious Death
Songs set to music, at the end.   A reproduction of the engraved title-page, and also of
two of the plates, will be found in this catalogue.   Douce, pp. 148-149.

MILAN, 1671.

MANNI (Gio. Bap.)   Varii e veri retratti della morte disegnati in
imagini ed espressi in essempii al peccatore duro di cuore, dal padre
Gio. Battista Marmi della compagnia de Giesu.   In *Milano*, 1671,
WITH FRONTISPIECE AND 29 CURIOUS COPPER PLATES OF DANCE OF
DEATH, 8vo., *full brown crushed morocco, gilt edges, by* BRADSTREET,
FINE COPY, RARE.

₊ A curious Italian issue.   A few of the plates are closely copied from Holbein, the
others are new and original.   Douce appears not to have seen this issue, but quotes one at
Venice dated 1669.   See Douce, p. 129.

RUSTING (S. van). Het Schouw-Toneel des Doods, waar op na't leeven vertoont wort de Doot op den Throon, etc., etc., heerschende over alle Staatten en Volkeren, etc., door Salomon van Rusting, Med. Doct. (The Show-place, or Theatre of Death, where his power is shown over all classes and conditions of men, etc.) *t'Amsterdam*, by Jan ten Hoorn, 1707, WITH ENGRAVED TITLE AND 30 PLATES, NEW AND CURIOUS, OF DANCE OF DEATH, 12mo., *full maroon calf, gilt top edges,* by ALFRED MATTHEWS, VERY FINE COPY, FIRST EDITION, ORIGINAL IMPRESSIONS, VERY RARE.

*** This is the first issue of the series prepared by Dr. van Rusting, some of which were in Low Dutch, and others in the German text. Many of the plates are very curious and clever, notably, "The Tight-Rope Dancer," and "The Skaters." A photograph of the title-page and one of the plates, taken from the 1735 edition, will be found herein. Douce, p. 131.

Another copy, same title and plates as above, with same text, 12mo., *full red morocco, gilt edges,* FINE AND CLEAN COPY, GOOD IMPRESSIONS, SCARCE.

*** As before stated, a reproduction of this engraved·title and one of the plates is given in this Catalogue.

RUSTING (S. van). Schau-platz des Todes, oder Todten-Tanz, in Kupfern und Versen vorgestellet, von Sal. van Rusting, Med. Doct. in Nieder-Teutscher Sprache, nun aber in Hoch-Teutscher mit nothigen Anmerkungen, herausgegeben von Joh. Georg. Meintel, etc., etc. (The Theatre or Show-place of Death, in Low German, but now in High German, copper-plates and verses, with notes by John Georg. Meintel, etc.) *Nürnberg*, 1736, WITH ENGRAVED TITLE, AND 30 ORIGINAL DESIGNS ILLUSTRATING THE DANCE OF DEATH, 8vo., *full Cambridge sheep, paneled sides,* by ALFRED MATTHEWS, TALL AND CLEAN COPY, FIRST IMPRESSIONS, RARE.

*** The first appearance in German, of a larger and more complete series of van Rusting's Low Dutch versions of earlier date as heretofore described. These plates are exactly the same designs, but newly engraved upon a larger scale, and the figures and dresses slightly modernized. As usual, the Holbein ideas pervade a number. Douce, pp. 131-132.

. . . . Another copy, exactly similar to above, at the end of which is bound in another work on Death, viz.: **BUQUOIT.** Krastiges Mittel wieder den Schrecken des Todes, WITH FINE FRONTISPIECE. *Franckfurt, 1733,* 2 vols. in 1, 8vo., *brown morocco, extra gilt edges,* by CHARLES SMITH, VERY FINE COPY.

*** This volume was formerly in the "Beckford" Collection at Fonthill.

PLATE VIII.

47

Todt zum Bapst.

Komm heiliger Vatter werther Mann/
Ein Vortantz müßt ihr mit mir han:
Der Ablaß euch nicht hilfft darvon/
Das zweyfach Creutz vnd dreyfach Kron.

Antwort.

HEilig war ich auff Erd genandt/
Ohn GOtt der höchst führt ich mein Stand;
Der Ablaß thät mir gar wol lohnen/
Nun wil der Todt mein nicht verschonen.

Todt

The Pope:

Mattheu Merian's Edition. Frankfort, 1649.

*

AMSTERDAM, 1741.

SANCTA CLARA (Abraham). De Kapelle der Dooden Of de Algemeene Doodenspeigel, etc., van Pater Abraham à Sancta Clara, etc. (The universal Mirror of Death, taken from the Chapel of the Dead, in which all men may see themselves laughing and weeping, etc.) *Te Amsterdam*, 1741, WITH FRONTISPIECE AND 68 CURIOUS AND ORIGINAL PLATES OF DANCE OF DEATH. Small 8vo., *full brown calf, gilt top edges, by* BRADSTREET, FINE COPY, CLEAR IMPRESSIONS, VERY SCARCE.

₊ The greater number of these engravings are new, and some can scarcely be called fitting to the subject treated; others show the Holbein features. "The Drunkard," "The Hen-pecked Husband," and "The Blind Beggar," are very cleverly done. Douce. pp. 151-152.

SCHELLENBERG'S DESIGNS.

WINTERTHUR, 1785.

SCHELLENBERG (J. R.) Freund Heins Erscheinungen in Holbein's manier, von J. R. Schellenberg. *Winterthur*, 1785, WITH FRONTISPIECE AND 24 CLEVER ORIGINAL DESIGNS OF A DEATH DANCE, 8vo., *polished calf, gilt top edges*, UNCUT, by FRANCIS BEDFORD, VERY FINE COPY, FIRST EDITION, RARE.

₊ A thoroughly original series. One of these plates represents a death by Balooning, (but lately invented). Another borders on the indecent. The frontispiece contains portraits of Voltaire, Frederick of Prussia, and others. A representation of one of the plates, "The Student," is herein given. This copy is from the library of the late distinguished London binder, Mr. Bedford.

M. RENTZ'S DESIGNS.

PASSAU-LINTZ, 1753.

RENTZ (M.) Geistliche Todts-Gedanchen bey allerhand Gemahlden und Tchildereyn in vorbildung Unterscheidlichen geschlechts, alters, standes, und wurdens persohnen sich des Todes, etc., etc. (The Spiritual Dance of Death in all kinds of pictures, whereby persons of every age, rank and sex, may be reminded of Death, first, put upon copper, and afterwards brought to light in Death's own colors, etc., etc.) *Passau-Lintz*, 1753, WITH 52 LARGE, FULL PAGE COPPER PLATES, ENTIRELY NEW AND STRIKING DESIGNS, ENGRAVED BY M. RENTZ, folio, *half morocco, cloth sides*, FIRST EDITION, ORIGINAL, CLEAR IMPRESSIONS, FINE, CLEAN COPY, RARE.

₊ These designs are upon a much larger and grander scale than usual, and exhibit marked originality and spirit. Occasional hints from Holbein are discovered in some of the pictures. This first edition in good state is rare, and not easily obtainable. Douce, pp. 152-153.

FREUND HEINS Wanderungen. *Gorlitz,* 1795. Small 8vo.,
boards, good, sound copy, SCARCE.

** Has a copper-plate frontispiece, an old man conversing with a grave-digger; also vignette, on title-page, engraved by Boettger. The text is a series of poems in German, relating to Death as connected with all the trades, professions, and dignities of men. Very quaint and curious. No other plates.

PLATE IX.

Title-Page:
Dr. Van Rusting's Series. Amsterdam, 1735.

*

Copies of the Basle Paintings.

MERIAN (M.)   Todten-Tantz, wie derselbe in der loblichen in der weitberühmpten Stadt Basel als ein Spiegel Menslicher Beschaffenheit ganz künstlich gemahlet zu sehen ist, etc.   Nach dem Original in Kupffer gebracht und heraus gegeben durch Matthaeum Merian den Eltern.   *Frankfurt,* Im Jar MDCXLIX., WITH ENGRAVED TITLE AND 42 COPPER PLATES OF THE BASLE DANCE OF DEATH, 4to, *half vellum,* FIRST EDITION, VERY RARE.

₊ Merian made these copies of the old paintings in Basle, early in the 17th century. Douce pronounces them the most complete and perfect of any.   There were several editions issued, some with French and some with German text.   In this issue the text is entirely German.   A photograph copy of the title-page, and also of one of the cuts, "The Pope," appears herewith.   Douce, p, 41.   Langlois, Tome II., pp. 176-181.

Another copy, similar to the above, WITH SAME TITLE, PLATES, ETC., issued by the heirs of Merian.   *Frankfurt,* 1696, 4to., *full purple morocco, gilt toolings, gilt top edges, by* ALFRED MATTHEWS, FINE COPY, CLEAR IMPRESSIONS.

MERIAN (M.)   La Danse des Morts, telle qu'on la voit depeinte dans la célèbre ville de Basle qui represente la fragilité de la vie humaine, comme dans un Miroir.   Enrichie de Tailles-douces, faites après l'original de la Peinture, etc., etc.   Imprimé à *Berlin,* aux dépens des Heritiers de l'Auteur, MDCXCVIII., WITH ENGRAVED TITLE AND 42 PLATES BY M. MERIAN, 4to., *full dark calf, gilt top edges, by* ALFRED MATTHEWS, FINE, CLEAR IMPRESSIONS, SCARCE.

₊ This is the first edition with French text throughout.   It was issued by the heirs of Merian.   The plates appear to be the same as in the earlier issues.

MERIAN'S PLATES,
COPIED AND ENGRAVED BY CHOVIN.

BASLE, 1744.

La Danse des Morts, comme elle est depeinte dans la louable et célèbre ville de Basle, pour servir d'un miroir de la nature humaine. Dessinée et Gravée sur l'original de feu Mr. Matthieu Merian, etc., etc. *A Basle,* chez Jean Rod. Im-Hoff. 1744, WITH TITLE AND 42 PLATES, AFTER MERIAN, BY CHOVIN, 4to, *paper covers,* REMARKABLE COPY, ENTIRELY UNCUT, AS FIRST ISSUED.

** It appears that Mons. Chovin, a French or Swiss engraver, has here copied the Merian plates. His name is found upon some of them. The text is in both French and German. This copy is noticeable as being in same condition as when published, even the top leaves remaining uncut, and plates very fresh and clean.

MERIAN'S PLATES.
CURIOUSLY BURLESQUED AND MODERNIZED.
LOCLE, 1788.

La Danse des Morts, pour servir de miroir à la nature humaine. Avec le costume dessiné à la moderne, et des vers à chaques figures. *Au Locle chez Sl. Girardet Libraire,* 1788, WITH FRONTISPIECE AND CURIOUS PLATES, AFTER MERIAN, 8vo., *half bound,* GOOD, SOUND COPY, CLEAN ORIGINAL IMPRESSIONS, VERY SCARCE.

** In this volume an unknown artist has copied the Merian plates, but has arranged the various figures in modern costumes, producing a very curious effect. Two of these figures have been copied in this Catalogue. The text is also in verses. At the end of the volume is a queer treatise, "L'Art de bien vivre et de bien mourir," (The Art of living and dying well), with an additional plate. It is a very scarce book, and difficult to procure. Douce, p. 42. Langlois, Tome II., pp. 177-181.

COPIES OF THE BASLE PAINTINGS,
ENGRAVED ON WOOD.
BASLE, 1796.

Der Todten=Tantz, wie derselbe in der Weitberühmten Stadt Basel als ein Spiegel menschlicher Beschaffenheit ganz Künstlich mit lebendigen Farben gemahlet nicht ohne nützliche verwunderung zu sehen ist. *Basel,* bey gebrüdern von Mechel, 1796, WITH 42 WOOD-CUTS COPIED AFTER THE BASLE PAINTINGS, AND ALSO AFTER HOLBEIN, 8vo., *half levant crushed morocco, gilt top edges,* UNCUT, by ALFRED MATTHEWS, FINE, CLEAN EXAMPLE, CLEAR IMPRESSIONS, VERY SCARCE.

** This seems to be a modern reprint of some cuts that possibly had been engraved in the latter 16th century. Upon one of the blocks is found the mark, G. S., and the date, 1576. Only a few of these wood-cuts are copies of the old paintings at Basle; the most of them are derived from the Holbein series. The text is in verses, and in the German language. Douce, pp. 40 and 41.

PLATE X.

Ver ..i Koorde-danſſer,

Die gek dient hier niet tot plyzier.

't Is zekerlyk geen Wisjewasje:
Ligt maakt hy eenig pasjen vals ;
En valt, op 't minste valsche pasje
Van boven neer, en breekt den hals .

The Rope-Dancer :
Van Rusting's Series. Amsterdam, 1735.

*

Another copy, same title. Small 4to, *half levant morocco, gilt top edges*, UNCUT, by ALFRED MATTHEWS.

₊ A modern reprint of the cuts, etc., of the 1706 edition above described, the cuts evidently newly engraved. Text in German and French.

RECENT REPRINT, BASLE, CIRCA 1860.

𝕿𝖔𝖉𝖊𝖓𝖙𝖆𝖓𝖟 𝖉𝖊𝖗 𝕾𝖙𝖆𝖉𝖙 𝕭𝖆𝖘𝖊𝖑, mit 42 Abbildungen, Deutschem, Englischem und Französ. text. *Basel, n. d., circa* 1860, WITH COPIES OF THE BASLE PAINTINGS, 8vo., *half sheep, gilt top edges,* UNCUT.

————

BASLE, 1858.

𝕿𝖔𝖉𝖊𝖓𝖙𝖆𝖓𝖟 𝖉𝖊𝖗 𝕾𝖙𝖆𝖉𝖙 𝕭𝖆𝖘𝖊𝖑. *Basel,* Otto Stuckert, 1858, WITH COPIES OF THE BASLE PAINTINGS. Small, square 12mo., *half morocco.*

₊ Two inexpensive modern issues, giving the Basle pictures, accompanied by interesting remarks, and text in German, French and English.

ⅅanſe ⅅacaƀre

EDITIONS COPIED AFTER THE EARLY DANSE MACABRE.

TROYES, 1728.

La Grande Danse Macabre des Hommes et des Femmes, ✓ renouvellée de vieux Gaulois en langage le plus poli de notre temps, etc. *Troyes, n. d.*, (1728), WITH 52 CURIOUS AND CRUDE CUTS OF THE EARLY DANSE MACABRE, 4to, *half morocco*, GOOD, SOUND COPY, SCARCE.

  ₊ The wood-cuts that illustrate this volume form one of the earliest representations of the Dance of Death, being originally engraved about 1480. Of the first editions issued in Paris, only one or two copies are known to exist. The text is in verses, or form of a dialogue.

MODERN RE-IMPRESSION ON VELLUM.

PARIS, CIRCA 1860.

Danse Macabre. Chorea ab eximio Macabro versibus alemanicis edita. et a Petro Desray trecacio quod a oratore nuper emendata. Parisiis, per magistrum Guidonem mercatorem pro Godeffrido de marnef ad intersignium pellicani in vico divi Iacobi commorati. Anno Domini quadringentesimo nonagesimo supra millesimum idibus octobris impressa. *Paris, n. d.*, (*circa* 1860), WITH CUTS COPIED FROM AN EARLY FRENCH DANSE MACABRE, 4to, *full red morocco*, PRINTED UPON VELLUM, VERY SCARCE.

  ₊ This is a scarce and curious re-impression by the Baron Plinski process, of the celebrated work, "La Danse Macabre," printed at Paris by De Marnef in 1490. Only a very few copies were printed upon vellum. The cuts are reproduced in a very masterly manner, and excellently printed.

PARIS, 1858.

La grant Danse Macabre des hõmes et des fẽmes, avec les ⋎ dis des trois mors et trois vifs, etc. *A Paris*, 1858, WITH COPIES OF THE DANSE MACABRE. Small 4to, *half cloth*, UNCUT.

  ₊ Modern reprint of an early 15th century French edition, reduced in size.

BORUP (T. L.) Det menneskelige Livs Flugt, eller Dode-Dands, beførget til sine Landsmaends Nytte og Fornøjelfe af Thomas Larsen Borup. (The Human Life's Flight, or Death-Dance, provided for his countrymen's use and pleasure by T. L. B.) *Kjobenhavn*, 1814, WITH 36 VERY CURIOUS ORIGINAL WOOD-CUTS, AFTER THE MANNER OF THE DANSE MACABRE, 4to, *half roan*, ENTIRELY UNCUT, TOP LEAVES UNOPENED, VERY SCARCE.

*** A curious version, not cited by the bibliographers. The text is in verses, and in the form of a dialogue between Death and various characters.

Edition with Burlesque Verses,

Lyons, 1702.

JAQUES-JAQUES. Le Faut-Mourir, et les excuses inutiles qu'on aporte à cette necessité. Augmenté de l'avocat nouvellement marié, et des pensées sur l'eternité. *Le tout en vers burlesques. A Lyon*, 1702, 8vo., *half calf*, SCARCE AND CURIOUS.

*** This work has no plates except a frontispiece, in which two Deaths, with other figures, are presenting themselves before the Pope.

' The text consists of a series of rhymes, after the manner of the early Danse Macabre. All conditions of mankind going to their death, and each reciting the most ridiculous and inappropriate excuses for their arriving at this inevitable result. Douce, (p. 26), quotes this as a very scarce and uncommon work.

Recent Reprint,

Paris, N. D.

La Dance Macabre, composée par Maistre Jehan Gerson, 1425. *Paris*, (WILLEM), *n. d.*, WITH FAC-SIMILE PLATES OF AN EARLY MANUSCRIPT OF THE DANSE MACABRE, 8vo., *half calf, gilt top edges*, UNCUT.

*** *Tiré à très-petit nombre sur papier de Hollande.* Epuisé.

PLATE XI.

The Physician—The Gentleman.

FROM

"*La Danse des Morts.*" *Au Locle, 1788.*

*

London Editions.

Rowlandson's Designs.
London, 1815-1816.

COMBE (Wm.) The English Dance of Death, a Poem from the designs of Thomas Rowlandson, with metrical illustrations by the author of "Doctor Syntax." *London*, (ACKERMANN), 1815-1816, WITH 74 FINELY COLORED AND SPIRITED PLATES, BY ROWLANDSON, 2 vols., Royal 8vo., *half russia*, GOOD, SOUND COPIES, ORIGINAL IMPRESSIONS, FIRST EDITION, VERY SCARCE.

₊ The clever and humorous Rowlandson found an ample and congenial field for his facile pencil in this subject, and he has given some remarkably curious and original ideas in his numerous plates, conveying a powerful moral lesson,—while the poetical text by Combe, is in thorough harmony with the artist's labors. This has become a very dear and costly edition, ranging in price from £9 to £15 Sterling. Douce, pp. 156-157.

Rowlandson's Designs.
London, 1817.

COMBE (Wm.) The English Dance of Life, a Poem with metrical illustrations, by William Combe, author of "Doctor Syntax." *London*, (ACKERMANN), 1817, WITH 26 HUMOROUS COLORED PLATES BY ROWLANDSON. Royal 8vo., *half russia*, FIRST EDITION, FINE ORIGINAL IMPRESSIONS, VERY SCARCE.

₊ Though this work might not properly be placed in this collection, as the skeleton Death is not present in the plates; yet, as it is a sequel to the Dance of Death, with Rowlandson's designs, it has seemed fitting to record it. The three volumes are generally sold in one set.

Van Assen's Designs.
London, 1825.

VAN ASSEN. The British Dance of Death, exemplified by a series of engravings from drawings by Van Assen, with explanatory and moral essays. *London, n. d.*, (circa 1825), WITH COLORED FRONTISPIECE BY CRUIKSHANK, AND 18 SEMI-HUMOROUS COLORED PLATES BY VAN ASSEN, 8vo., *black morocco, gilt edges*, FINE COPY, VERY SCARCE.

₊ These drawings are all original, and very neatly engraved and tinted. Douce, pp. 158-159.

37

DAGLEY'S ETCHINGS.
LONDON, 1826.

DAGLEY (R.) Death's Doings, consisting of numerous original compositions in prose and verse, principally intended as illustrations of 24 plates, designed and etched by R. Dagley, author of "Select Gems from the Antique," etc. *London,* 1826, WITH FRONTISPIECE AND 24 ORIGINAL DESIGNS BY DAGLEY, 8vo., *half calf,* GOOD, CLEAR IMPRESSIONS, SCARCE.

₊ This work is highly praised by Douce, p. 157. Some of the best writers of the day contributed to the text.

HULL'S DRAWINGS.
LONDON, 1827.

HULL (E.) Death's Ramble, Illustrations of. A series of seven colored drawings in stone by Edward Hull, taken from the Whims and Oddities of Tom. Hood. *London, n. d.,* (circa 1827), WITH 7 COLORED PLATES BY HULL. Large 4to, *half morocco,* SCARCE.

PLATE XII.

The Student:

BY

Schellenberg   Winterthur, 1785.

＊

𝕯𝖎𝖛𝖊𝖗𝖋𝖊 𝕰𝖉𝖎𝖙𝖎𝖔𝖓𝖘.

Two Curious Works in which the Subject is Introduced.

Dilingen, 1621.

WALASSER (Adam). Kunst wol zu sterben. Ein gar nutzliches hochnothwendiges Büchlein, auss heyliger Schrifft und alten bewehrten Lehrern, mit sonderm fleisz gezogen, und mit schönen Exempeln und Figuren gezieret. Gedruckt *zu Dilingen*, 1621, WITH UPWARDS OF 20 VERY CURIOUS WOOD-CUTS, AFTER THE OLD BLOCK BOOK, "ARS MORIENDI," AND A SERIES OF SMALL DANCE OF DEATH CUTS UPON ONE PAGE. Small 8vo., *in the original stamped hogskin binding, with metal clasps,* CLEAN, PERFECT COPY, VERY RARE.

*** On one page of this work is found a series of very small cuts in which the Dance of Death is portrayed in several curious and comical forms, all new and original. The work is very rare. The binding of this copy and the old wood-blocks representing death-bed scenes, are most curious and interesting. The cuts were evidently engraved during the 15th or 16th century. Douce, pp. 173-174, alludes to an earlier issue of this work dated 1569, and describes the cuts.

Strasburg, 1744.

STEINHAUER (Ant.) Vado Mori, das ist Bereitschaft zum Tod, oder der weg alles fleisches, durch eine ordentliche Todten-Procession, etc. *Strasburg und Augspurg*, 1744, WITH CURIOUS FRONTISPIECE OF DEATHS, ETC., 8vo., *boards*, SCARCE.

*** A very curious work in German and Latin text, in which all classes of mankind hold a dialogue in rhyme or verse with Death. There are no plates except the frontispiece.

Eglin's Copies of Von Wyl's Paintings.

Lucerne, 1843.

EGLIN. Todtentanz oder Spiegel menschlicher Hinfälligkeit in acht Abbildungen, welche, von Von Wyl gemalt, im ehemaligen Jesuitenkloster in Luzern aufbewahrt werden, mit Deutschem und Französischem Texte. *Luzern*, 1843, WITH 8 FINE LITHOGRAPHS, COPIES OF VON WYL'S PAINTINGS, BY EGLIN. Oblong folio, *half bound, cloth*, EPUISÉ.

*** Jacques de Wyl, about 1620-1630, painted in oil a Dance of Death, entirely original, portions of which, we believe, are still preserved in the library at Luzerne. The above work contains faithful and spirited copies of these paintings.

RETHEL (Alfred). Auch ein Todentanz, mit erklärendem Texte von R. Reinick, etc. *Leipzig, n. d.*, (circa 1849), WITH 6 FULL-PAGE WOOD-CUTS, DESIGNED BY RETHEL. Oblong 4to, *cloth, boards*, GOOD, CLEAN IMPRESSIONS.

₊ Rethel's very powerful and bold designs were inspired by the civil wars of 1848. They are handled in a masterly manner and present the Dance of Death in an original form not before attempted.

MODERN REPRINTS OF HOLBEIN'S
ALPHABET OF DEATH.

L'Alphabet de la Mort de Hans Holbein, par Anatole de Montaiglon. *Paris*, (TROSS), 1856, WITH BEAUTIFUL WOOD-CUT COPIES, BORDERS, INITIALS, ETC., AFTER THE STYLE OF THE EARLY BOOKS OF HOURS, 8vo., *half morocco, gilt top edges*, LARGE PAPER, UNCUT.

————

Another Copy. Italian Text, same plates. *Paris*, (TROSS), 1856, 8vo., *half vellum, gilt edges.*

Trois Danses des Morts. Soixante-douze gravures en bois. EPREUVES D'ARTISTE. *Paris*, (TROSS), 1856, *exemplaire sur papier de Chine fort.* Small 8vo., *half calf, gilt top edges*, UNCUT, RARE.

₊ Artist proofs of the Holbein Death Alphabet, also of figures of the Dance of Death taken from the French Horæ, or Books of Hours, printed early in the Fifteenth Century.

☞ Only 50 copies printed on Chinese paper.

PLATE XIII.

Other Works in this Library

An Illuminated Manuscript upon Vellum, of the 15th Century, contains a beautiful miniature of three youths, upon horseback, elegantly attired, accosted by three skeletons. "LE TROIS MORTS ET LES TROIS VIFS."

"THE NUREMBERG CHRONICLE," printed by Ant. Koburger, in *Nuremberg*, 1493. Folio.

"BRANDT'S STULTIFERA NAVIS," (Ship of Fools), printed by J. B. de Olpe. *Basle*, 1497. 4to.

"HEURES À L'USAIGE DE ROME," printed by T. Kerver. *Paris*, 1502. 8vo. (☞ A reproduction of one of these plates is given in this Catalogue.)

"HEURES À L'USAIGE DE TOU," printed by Guill. Godard. *Paris*, 1515. Large 8vo.

"HEURES À L'USAIGE DE ROME," printed by Gillet Hardouin. *Paris* 1518. 8vo.

"RUESNERI, N.—EMBLEMATUM." *Frankfort*, 1581. 4to.

"BOISSARDI.—EMBLEMATUM LIBER." *Frankfort*, 1593. 4to.

"BOISSARDI.—THEATRUM VITÆ HUMANÆ." *Frankfort*, 1596. 4to.

"PASSE CRISP. DE.—ANTHROPOMORPHOSE EIKONES." *Coloniæ*, 1599. Small Folio.

"TYPOTIUS.—SYMBOLA DIVINA." *Frankfort*, 1601. Folio.

"VŒNII OTHO.—EMBLEMATA HORATIANA." *Antwerp*, 1607. 4to.

"ROLLENHAGIUS.—NUCLEUS EMBLEMATUM." *Coloniæ*, 1611–1613. Small 4to.

"DAVID.—VIRIDICUS CHRISTIANUS." *Antwerp*, 1606. 4to.

"MUSART.—ADOLESCENS ACADEMICUS." *Duaci*, 1633. 12mo.

"DE CHERTABLON.—MANIERE DE SE BIEN PREPARER À LA MORT." *Anvers*, 1700. 4to. (☞ A plate from this work is reproduced in this Catalogue.)

"ALCIATI.—EMBLEMATA," numerous editions. 1531–1661.

"QUARLE'S EMBLEMS." *London*, 1777. 12mo.

"Till the slow sea rise and the sheer cliff crumble,

  Till the terrace and meadow the deep gulfs drink,

Till the strength of the waves of the high tides humble

  The fields that lessen, the rocks that shrink;

Here now in his triumph, where all things falter,

  Stretched out in the spoils that his own hand spread,

As a god self-slain on his own strange altar,

  Death Lies Dead."

—Swinburne.

The last enemy that shall be destroyed
is Death.—*1 Cor. xv., xxvi.*

Christ's Triumph:
Meyer's Edition. Zurich. 1650.

*

www.ingramcontent.com/pod-product-compliance
Lightning Source LLC
Chambersburg PA
CBHW021627270326
41931CB00008B/904